Potluck
FOR ALL OCCASIONS

Publications
International Ltd.

Favorite Brand Name Recipes at www.fbnr.com

Special thanks to the Campbell's Kitchen, Lucinda Ayers, Vice President, and Catherine Marschean-Spivak, Group Manager.

Photography on pages 9, 11, 13, 25, 29, 31, 37, 43, 45, 47, 49, 53, 65, 67, 69, 81, 89 and 91 by Stephen Hamilton Photographics, Inc., Chicago.

Pictured on the front cover: Turkey and Stuffing Casserole *(page 36)*.
Pictured on the back cover (clockwise from top): Tomato Soup Spice Cupcakes *(page 90),* Black Bean Salsa Dip with Vegetables *(page 8)* and Salsa Pork Braise *(page 28)*.

ISBN-13: 978-1-4127-2463-0
ISBN-10: 1-4127-2463-5

Manufactured in China.

8 7 6 5 4 3 2 1

Microwave Cooking: Microwave ovens vary in wattage. Use the cooking times as guidelines and check for doneness before adding more time.

Preparation/Cooking Times: Preparation times are based on the approximate amount of time required to assemble the recipe before cooking, baking, chilling or serving. These times include preparation steps such as measuring, chopping and mixing. The fact that some preparations and cooking can be done simultaneously is taken into account. Preparation of optional ingredients and serving suggestions is not included.

contents

Campbell's®
Potluck
FOR ALL OCCASIONS

A potluck dinner is a very popular way to entertain family and friends. It's an informal, fun and easy get-together, where everyone contributes a dish and shares in the cooking. But whether you're hosting a potluck or attending one, there is some planning involved. Campbell's *Potluck for All Occasions* will show you how to plan a potluck dinner, teach you how to transport food safely and provide dozens of recipes that will be just perfect for your next potluck occasion.

Planning Your Potluck

Here are some steps to ensure that your potluck party is fun, organized and successful:

■ A potluck is one of those times when it's perfectly acceptable, and practically expected, to ask each guest to bring a specific dish or a dish in a specific category; after all, you don't want to end up with one casserole and half a dozen desserts. Although a potluck can certainly be a random assortment of dishes, you may want to plan a menu, if only in general terms, so that you can be sure your guests will bring dishes that cover all the bases: appetizers, salads, main dishes, side dishes, breads, desserts and beverages.

■ After you've planned a menu, write the guest list, and decide what each guest should bring. Make a specific request—chicken casserole, or fudge, for instance—or a more general one—a main dish or a salad. Or, if you'd like the guest to decide, tell them what you need and ask what they'd be comfortable with. We all have a friend or a family member who loves to cook and bring his or her specialty dish to every gathering, so why not ask him or her for that dish if it fits your menu? On the other hand, we also all know people who just don't cook; ask them to bring beverages, ice, napkins or flowers for the table.

■ As the host, you might want to consider providing the appetizers so that early arrivers don't have to wait on a guest to bring them. Likewise, you might also want to provide some basic beverages, such as coffee, tea, wine, beer or soft drinks, plus ice, and ask a guest to bring any special drinks.

■ Theme potlucks are fun and even easier to plan than a regular potluck. For a Mexican potluck, for example, you could furnish the beverages—a Sangria punch, say, or makings for Margaritas—and guests could provide the salsa, taco fillings, cheese and flan. For a Thanksgiving potluck, the host is usually expected to cook the turkey since it's not a simple dish to transport; guests can provide all of the traditional side dishes. For a Fourth of July barbecue, you could provide the burgers and hot dogs; guests can provide the potato salad, buns, baked beans and cupcakes.

Preparing Your House

If you're hosting a potluck, there are a few things you can do to get ready for your guests:

■ Set the table, and/or organize the buffet. Set the buffet in a logical order: a stack of dinner plates first, then the food, then flatware wrapped in napkins at the end. Leave space along the front of the buffet for people to put their plates down while they're serving themselves.

■ Bring out some serving platters and utensils, just in case guests forget to bring them. Make some space in your refrigerator so there's a place to store cold dishes until it's time to eat. Likewise, preheat the oven to about 350°F. in case anything needs to be reheated or kept hot.

■ Organize beverages in an area separate from the dining table or buffet; coffee and dessert should be placed on a separate table, too.

■ Serve the appetizers just as guests are arriving.

Taking a Covered Dish

When you're taking food to a potluck, remember these tips:

■ Select a dish that can be prepared in advance.

■ Be considerate of your host: Don't plan to cook or bake your food in your host's kitchen. Bring a dish that doesn't require anything more than a quick reheat in the oven or microwave.

■ Unless it's a sitdown dinner, guests will probably be juggling a plate and a drink, so stick with foods that are easy to eat with just a fork and don't require cutting with a knife.

■ Select food that's portable and easy to transport: Casseroles, chili, salads, breads, cookies, bars and cupcakes are popular potluck foods because of their transportability.

Packing Up

Plastic lidded storage containers are best for transporting potluck foods such as salads, side dishes and desserts. Appetizers can usually be plated and covered with aluminum foil. Most casseroles can be transported in the dishes in which they were prepared—just be sure to cover them with lids or heavy-duty aluminum foil. To keep them warm, try wrapping them in bath towels before loading them in the car.

■ Place containers into a cardboard box or in paper grocery bags with handles for easy transport in and out of the car.

■ Label casseroles and containers with your name and phone number (on masking tape on the bottom of the containers) in case you forget and accidentally leave them behind. Better yet, bring food in a disposable container or one that doesn't have to be returned.

■ Give your host a break, and pack whatever utensils you'll need to serve your food: ladles, meat forks, serving spoons, knives, cake servers and so on.

Food Safety

When food has been prepared in advance, transported and allowed to sit while guests are having drinks and appetizers, the likelihood of bacterial growth can increase. Here are some things you can do to reduce the risk of foodborne illness:

■ Keep hot foods hot (greater than 140°F.) and cold foods cold (less than 40°F.).

■ Prepare food the same day as the potluck, preferably within three hours of serving. If that's not possible, cook the food in plenty of time so that it can be thoroughly chilled. Then, transport the food in a cooler with ice or ice packs and reheat before serving.

■ Pack up cold foods directly from the refrigerator in coolers that have been chilled with ice water or ice for at least an hour. Empty the cooler before adding the cold food. Or place frozen gel packs or ice in the bottom of a cooler or thermal food tote. Place food on top; place more ice packs or ice on top of the food. (Resealable plastic food storage bags filled with ice cubes make good homemade ice packs.) Keep the cooler closed until serving time.

■ In hot weather, transport the cooler inside your air-conditioned car instead of in the hot trunk. In cold months, the trunk is the better place.

■ Pack hot foods directly from the oven or stove into preheated insulated containers or food totes. To preheat an insulated container, fill it with boiling water and let it sit for a few minutes. Drain and immediately fill it with piping hot food. Keep the container closed until serving time.

THE TWO-HOUR RULE

Refrigerate or freeze prepared food and leftovers within two hours. Discard food that's been left out longer than two hours in what experts call "The Danger Zone"—between 40°F. and 140°F.

Appetizers to Go

Get your party started with these easy, packable appetizers

Black Bean Salsa Dip with Vegetables

MAKES 1¾ CUPS

PREP
5 minutes

REFRIGERATE
2 hours

1   can (10¾ ounces) Campbell's® Condensed Black Bean Soup

½   cup Pace® Chunky Salsa

     Shredded Cheddar cheese

     Sliced pitted ripe olives

     Sliced green onions

     Sour cream

     Tortilla chips **or assorted cut-up fresh vegetables**

1. Stir the soup and salsa in a small bowl. Refrigerate at least 2 hours or until the flavors are blended.

2. Top with the cheese, olives, onions and sour cream. Serve with the chips or vegetables for dipping.

To serve warm: Heat soup and salsa over medium heat until it's hot, stirring often.

Spicy Roasted Red Pepper Dip

PREP
25 minutes

15 Pepperidge Farm® Hearty Wheat Crackers

1 jar (24 ounces) roasted sweet peppers, drained

1½ cups walnuts

1 tablespoon lemon juice

1 tablespoon honey

¾ teaspoon ground cumin

1 package (14 ounces) Pepperidge Farm® Hearth Fired Artisan Bread, any variety

¼ cup olive oil

LEFTOVER TIP

Serve dip with cooked tortellini, chicken strips or breaded mozzarella sticks for dipping.

1. Put the crackers, peppers and walnuts in a food processor. Cover and process until the mixture is puréed.

2. With the machine running, add the juice, honey and cumin.

3. Bake and cool the bread according to the package directions. Diagonally cut the bread into 1-inch-thick slices. Brush the bread slices with oil. Grill or broil the bread as directed below. Serve with the dip.

To Grill: Lightly oil the grill and heat the grill to medium-high. Place the bread on the grill. Grill the bread for about 4 minutes or until lightly browned, turning the bread at a 90° angle (making crisscross grill marks) halfway through cooking.

To Broil: Heat the broiler. Place the bread slices on a baking sheet. Broil the bread so the top is 7 inches from the heat for 2 minutes or until lightly browned, turning over halfway through cooking.

Spicy Shrimp Cocktail Spread

MAKES 6 CUPS

PREP
10 minutes

CHILL
6 hours

1 envelope unflavored gelatin
¼ cup cold water
1 can (10¾ ounces) Campbell's® Condensed Tomato Soup
1 package (8 ounces) cream cheese, cut into pieces
1 cup mayonnaise
2 tablespoons prepared horseradish
1 teaspoon hot pepper sauce
2 stalks celery, chopped (about 1 cup)
1 large onion, diced (about 1 cup)
3 cans (4 to 6 ounces **each**) baby shrimp, drained
Assorted Pepperidge Farm® Crackers
Chopped parsley

TRANSPORTING TIP

Take along the shrimp spread in the 6-cup mold and unmold onto a serving plate after arriving at the potluck.

1. Sprinkle the gelatin over the water in a 2-quart saucepan. Let stand for 3 minutes or until the gelatin softens.

2. Stir the soup into the saucepan. Cook and stir over medium heat until the gelatin dissolves. Add the cream cheese and stir until the cheese melts. Remove from the heat.

3. Spoon the soup mixture, mayonnaise, horseradish, hot pepper sauce, celery, onion and shrimp into an electric food processor or blender. Cover and process until smooth. Pour mixture into a 6 cup mold. Cover and refrigerate for at least 6 hours or until the mixture is firm.

4. Invert and unmold the mixture onto serving plate. Sprinkle with the parsley. Serve with the crackers.

12 APPETIZERS TO GO

Layered Pizza Dip

PREP
10 minutes

BAKE
15 minutes

COOL
5 minutes

1 cup part-skim ricotta cheese

½ cup chopped pepperoni

1 cup shredded mozzarella cheese (4 ounces)

1 cup Prego® Italian Sauce, any variety

Pepperidge Farm® Garlic Bread, any variety, heated according to package directions or Pepperidge Farm® Crackers, any variety

---

EASY SUBSTITUTION TIP

Substitute or add any of the following toppings for the pepperoni: sliced pitted olives, sliced mushrooms, chopped sweet peppers or chopped onions.

---

1. Spread the ricotta cheese in an even layer in a 9-inch pie plate. Top with ¼ **cup** of the pepperoni and ½ **cup** of the mozzarella cheese. Carefully spread the sauce over the cheese. Sprinkle with the remaining pepperoni and mozzarella cheese.

2. Bake at 375°F. for 15 minutes or until hot. Let cool for 5 minutes.

3. Serve with the garlic bread or crackers for dipping.

Sack 'em Salsa

PREP
5 minutes

1½ cups Pace® Chunky Salsa

1 fluid ounce (2 tablespoons) tequila (optional)

½ cup sliced pitted ripe olives

¼ cup chopped fresh cilantro leaves

Sour cream

Tortilla chips

1. Mix the salsa, tequila, olives and cilantro in a 3-cup serving bowl. Top with the sour cream.

2. Serve with the chips for dipping.

Layered Pizza Dip

Hummus

PREP
25 minutes

STAND
1 hour

1 can (about 15 ounces) chickpeas (garbanzo beans), rinsed and drained

¼ cup Swanson® Vegetable Broth (Regular **or** Certified Organic)

1 cup prepared tahini

½ cup lemon juice

4 cloves garlic, minced

2 tablespoons olive oil

1 package (14 ounces) Pepperidge Farm® Hearth Fired Artisan Bread, any variety

¼ cup olive oil

1. Put the beans and broth in a food processor. Cover and process until the mixture is puréed.

2. Add the tahini, juice and garlic. Blend until the mixture turns lighter in color. With the machine running add the oil and blend until smooth. Spoon the hummus into a small bowl. Season to taste. Cover and let stand for at least 1 hour or until the flavors are blended.

3. Bake and cool the bread according to the package directions. Diagonally cut the bread into 1-inch-thick slices. Brush the bread slices with oil. Grill or broil the bread as directed below. Serve with the dip.

To Grill: Lightly oil the grill and heat the grill to medium-high. Place the bread on the grill. Grill the bread for about 4 minutes or until lightly browned, turning the bread at a 90° angle (making crisscross grill marks) halfway through cooking.

To Broil: Heat the broiler. Place the bread slices on a baking sheet. Broil the bread so the top is 7 inches from the heat for 2 minutes or until lightly browned, turning over halfway through cooking.

Salsa-Ranch Dip

¾   cup Pace® Chunky Salsa **or** Picante Sauce

1   container (16 ounces) sour cream

1   package (1.0 ounce) ranch dip mix

   Tortilla chips **or** assorted cut-up fresh vegetables

PREP
5 minutes

REFRIGERATE
1 hour

1. Stir the salsa, sour cream and dip mix in a small bowl.

2. Refrigerate for at least 1 hour until the flavors are blended.

3. Serve with chips or vegetables for dipping.

Walnut-Cheddar Ball

MAKES 2 CUPS

PREP
20 minutes

REFRIGERATE
2 hours

2 cups shredded Cheddar cheese (8 ounces)

½ cup walnuts, finely chopped

¼ cup mayonnaise

1 medium green onion, chopped (about 2 tablespoons)

1 tablespoon Dijon-style mustard

1 teaspoon Worcestershire sauce

¼ cup chopped fresh parsley

1 tablespoon paprika

Pepperidge Farm® Cracker Quartet **or** Cracker Trio Entertaining Collection Cracker Assortment

HOLIDAY TIP

Shape the cheese mixture into a candy cane, tree or star shape for an alternative presentation.

1. Stir the cheese, walnuts, mayonnaise, green onion, mustard and Worcestershire in a 1½-quart bowl until the ingredients are mixed.

2. Mix the parsley and paprika on a piece of wax paper. Shape the cheese mixture into a ball, then roll in the parsley mixture to coat. Wrap in plastic wrap. Refrigerate for 2 hours or until firm.

3. Unwrap the cheese ball and place on a serving plate. Serve with the crackers.

Chili Cheese Dip

MAKES 2¾ CUPS

PREP
5 minutes

MICROWAVE
3 to 4 minutes

1 can (11¼ ounces) Campbell's® Condensed Fiesta Chili Beef with Beans Soup

¾ cup sour cream

¾ cup shredded Cheddar **or** Monterey Jack cheese

Sliced green onions

Sliced pitted ripe olives (optional)

Tortilla chips

1. Spread the soup in a 9-inch microwavable pie plate. Top with the sour cream and cheese.

2. Microwave on HIGH for 3 to 4 minutes or until the cheese melts. Top with the green onions and olives, if desired. Serve with the chips for dipping.

Walnut-Cheddar Ball

Sausage Bites

THAW
40 minutes

PREP
20 minutes

BAKE
15 minutes

½ of a 17.3-ounce package Pepperidge Farm® Frozen Puff
   Pastry Sheets (1 sheet)

½ pound bulk pork sausage

1. Thaw the pastry sheet at room temperature for 40 minutes or until it's easy to handle. Heat the oven to 400°F.

2. Unfold the pastry on a lightly floured surface. Roll into a 12×10-inch rectangle. Cut into 3 (3-inch) strips.

3. Divide the sausage into thirds. Roll each into a cylinder the length of the pastry. Place on the edge of the pastry strip. Starting at the long side, roll up. Press the edges to seal.

4. Cut each roll into 12 (1-inch) slices. Place slices, cut-side down, 1½ inches apart, on 2 baking sheets. Bake for 15 minutes or until golden and sausage is cooked through. Serve warm.

Make Ahead: Cut into slices and place on baking sheet. Freeze. When frozen, store in plastic bag for up to 1 month. To bake, preheat oven to 400°F. Place frozen slices on baking sheets. Bake for 20 minutes or until golden and sausage is done.

> **EASY SUBSTITUTION TIP**
>
> *Substitute sweet or hot Italian pork sausage (casing removed) for the bulk pork sausage.*

Honey Mustard Chicken Bites

PREP
15 minutes

BAKE
15 minutes

1½ pounds skinless, boneless chicken breasts, cut into 1-inch
    pieces

1 jar (12 ounces) refrigerated honey mustard salad dressing

2 cups Pepperidge Farm® Herb Seasoned Stuffing, crushed

2 tablespoons orange juice

1. Dip the chicken into ¾ **cup** of the dressing, then coat with the stuffing.

2. Put the chicken on a baking sheet. Bake at 400°F. for 15 minutes or until the chicken is cooked through.

3. Stir the remaining dressing and orange juice in a 1-quart saucepan over medium heat. Cook and stir until it's hot. Serve with the chicken for dipping.

> **TIME-SAVING TIP**
>
> *To microwave dip, mix remaining dressing and orange juice in microwavable bowl. Microwave on HIGH for 1 minute or until hot.*

Hot Artichoke Dip

1 cup mayonnaise

1 cup sour cream

1 can (14 ounces) artichoke hearts, drained and chopped

¼ cup chopped roasted sweet peppers

¼ cup grated Parmesan cheese

1 can (2.8 ounces) French fried onions (1⅓ cups)

Assorted Pepperidge Farm® Crackers

PREP
10 minutes

BAKE
30 minutes

1. Heat the oven to 375°F. Mix the mayonnaise, sour cream, artichokes, peppers, cheese and ⅔ **cup** onions in 9-inch pie plate or 1-quart baking dish. Bake for 25 minutes or until hot.

2. Top with the remaining onions. Bake for 5 minutes more or until golden.

3. Serve with the crackers for dipping.

Artichoke and Spinach Swirls

PREP
45 minutes

BAKE
15 minutes

COOL
15 minutes

1   package (17.3 ounces) Pepperidge Farm® Frozen Puff Pastry
    Sheets (2 sheets)

½   cup mayonnaise

½   cup grated Parmesan cheese

1   teaspoon onion powder

1   teaspoon garlic powder

½   teaspoon ground black pepper

1   package (10 ounces) frozen chopped spinach, thawed
    and well drained

1   can (14 ounces) artichoke hearts, drained and chopped

1. Thaw the pastry sheets at room temperature for 40 minutes or until they're easy to handle. Heat the oven to 400°F. Line 2 baking sheets with parchment paper or spray with vegetable cooking spray.

2. Stir the mayonnaise, cheese, onion powder, garlic powder, black pepper, spinach and artichokes in a small bowl until the ingredients are mixed.

3. Unfold **1** pastry sheet on a lightly floured surface. With the short side facing you, spread **half** of the spinach mixture on the pastry to within 1 inch of the edges. Starting at the short sides, roll up like a jelly roll. Repeat with remaining pastry sheet and spinach mixture.

4. Cut each roll into 20 (½-inch) slices. Place 2 inches apart on prepared baking sheets.

5. Bake for 15 minutes or until golden. Remove from the baking sheets and cool slightly on a wire rack. Serve warm or at room temperature.

Baked Drumsticks Dijon

24 chicken drumsticks (about 8 pounds)

3½ cups Swanson® Chicken Broth (Regular, Natural Goodness™ **or** Certified Organic)

1 cup Dijon-style mustard

1 cup Italian-seasoned dry bread crumbs

PREP
10 minutes

MARINATE
4 hours

BAKE
1 hour

1. Put the chicken in a single layer between **2** (15×10-inch) disposable aluminum foil bakeware pans.

2. Stir the broth and mustard in a medium bowl. Pour the broth mixture over the chicken and turn to coat. Sprinkle the bread crumbs over the chicken. Refrigerate for 4 hours.

3. Bake at 375°F. for 1 hour or until the chicken is cooked through. Serve immediately or let stand 30 minutes to serve at room temperature, using the pan juices as a dipping sauce.

Party-Friendly Fare

Casseroles and main dishes that go

from stove to buffet table

EZ Stuffed Shells

PREP
10 minutes

COOK
20 minutes

1 pound ground beef

1 jar (1 pound 10 ounces) Prego® Traditional Italian Sauce

¾ cup grated Parmesan cheese

1 package (12 ounces) jumbo shell-shaped pasta, cooked and drained

1 cup shredded part-skim mozzarella cheese (4 ounces)

TRANSPORTING TIP

Transfer the meat mixture into a thermal container and the heated sauce into another thermal container. Fill the shells at the potluck.

1. Cook the beef in a 10-inch skillet over medium-high heat until well browned, stirring frequently to break up meat. Pour off any fat.

2. Stir **2 cups** of the sauce and ½ **cup** of the Parmesan cheese into the skillet. Cook for 5 minutes or until the meat mixture thickens.

3. Heat the remaining sauce in a 1-quart saucepan over medium heat, stirring often.

4. Spoon the meat mixture into the pasta shells and place on a serving platter.

5. Serve the filled shells with heated sauce, mozzarella and remaining Parmesan cheese for topping.

Shortcut Paella

PREP
15 minutes

COOK
25 minutes

STAND
5 minutes

1   tablespoon vegetable oil

2   cups **uncooked** regular long-grain white rice

4   cups Swanson® Chicken Broth (Regular, Natural Goodness™ **or** Certified Organic), heated

1   cup Pace® Chunky Salsa

1   teaspoon ground turmeric

1   pound turkey kielbasa, sliced

1   package (12 ounces) frozen shelled and deveined small cooked shrimp, thawed (2 cups)

1   package (about 10 ounces) refrigerated cooked chicken breast strips (2 cups)

1. Heat the oil in a 12-inch skillet over medium heat. Add the rice and cook for 30 seconds, stirring constantly. Stir the broth, salsa and turmeric into the skillet. Heat to a boil. Reduce the heat to low. Cover the skillet and cook for 15 minutes.

2. Stir the kielbasa, shrimp and chicken into the skillet. Cover and cook for 5 minutes more or until the rice is tender and most of the liquid is absorbed. Let the paella stand for 5 minutes before serving.

Salsa Pork Braise

PREP
15 minutes

BAKE
2 hours

STAND
10 minutes

2 tablespoons olive oil

4 pounds boneless pork shoulder butt

2 large carrots, chopped (about 1 cup)

3 cloves garlic, chopped

1 jar (24 ounces) Pace® Chunky Salsa

2 cups Swanson® Chicken Broth (Regular, Natural Goodness™
   or Certified Organic)

2 tablespoons tomato paste

1 tablespoon chili powder

   Cooked rice

MAKE AHEAD TIP

Pork can be made 1 day ahead. Cool and refrigerate. Reheat over medium heat before serving.

---

1. Heat **1 tablespoon** of the oil in an oven-safe 6-quart saucepot over medium-high heat. Add the pork and cook until it's well browned on all sides. Remove the pork and set aside.

2. Add remaining oil to the saucepot. Reduce the heat to medium. Add the carrots and garlic and cook until tender.

3. Stir the salsa, broth, tomato paste and chili powder into the saucepot. Heat to a boil. Return the pork to the saucepot and reduce the heat to low.

4. Cover the saucepot and bake at 350°F. for 2 hours or until the meat is fork-tender.

5. Remove the roast from the saucepot to a cutting board and let it stand for 10 minutes. Thinly slice the pork and return meat to the saucepot. Serve over rice.

Shredded Pork Sandwiches: Using 2 forks, shred the pork. Return the shredded pork to the saucepot. Divide the pork and sauce mixture among round sandwich rolls.

28 PARTY-FRIENDLY FARE

Italian-Style Sampler Supper

MAKES 8 SERVINGS

PREP
10 minutes

COOK
10 minutes

EASY SUBSTITUTION TIP

*Offer an assortment
of garnishes, such as
sliced ripe olives, sliced
mushrooms, chopped
pepperoni **and/or**
chopped green onion
to customize the dipping
sauce.*

16   (1 ounce **each**) cooked meatballs

16   breaded cooked chicken nuggets **or** tenders

16   frozen breaded mozzarella cheese sticks

1   loaf Pepperidge Farm® Garlic Bread, any variety

2   cups Prego® Traditional Italian Sauce

½   cup shredded mozzarella cheese

1. Heat the meatballs, chicken, mozzarella sticks and garlic bread according to the package directions. Slice the bread.

2. Heat the sauce in a 2-quart saucepan over medium heat, stirring often. Remove from the heat and stir in the cheese. Spoon into a serving bowl. Serve with the meatballs, chicken, mozzarella sticks and garlic bread strips for dipping.

Spiral Ham with Mango Salsa

PREP
15 minutes

BAKE
2 hours

1 tablespoon butter

1 medium onion, chopped (about ½ cup)

1½ cups Swanson® Chicken Broth (Regular, Natural Goodness™ **or** Certified Organic)

½ cup mango juice **or** nectar

1 package (6 ounces) dried mango, coarsely chopped

⅓ cup packed brown sugar

2 medium green onions, chopped (about ¼ cup), optional

9-pound fully cooked bone-in **or** 6-pound fully cooked boneless spiral cut ham

EASY SUBSTITUTION TIP

Substitute chopped fresh cilantro leaves for the green onions.

1. Heat the butter in a 2-quart saucepan over medium-high heat. Add the onion and cook until it's tender. Stir in the broth, mango juice, dried mango and brown sugar. Heat to a boil. Reduce the heat to low. Cook for 10 minutes or until the mixture thickens. Let cool slightly.

2. Place a strainer over a medium bowl. Pour the broth mixture through the strainer. Reserve the strained broth mixture to glaze the ham. Put the mango mixture in a small bowl. Stir in the green onions, if desired to make the salsa. Cover and refrigerate until serving time.

3. Place the ham in a 17×11-inch roasting pan and cover loosely with foil. Bake at 325°F. for 1½ hours. Remove the foil. Spoon the broth mixture over the ham. Bake for 30 minutes more or until internal temperature of the ham reaches 140°F., basting the ham frequently with the pan drippings. Serve the ham with the mango salsa.

Vegetable Lasagna

PREP
15 minutes

BAKE
50 minutes

STAND
10 minutes

2 cans (10¾ ounces **each**) Campbell's® Condensed Cream of Broccoli Soup (Regular **or** 98% Fat Free)

1½ cups milk

Vegetable cooking spray

1 tablespoon butter

3¾ cups sliced mushrooms (about 10 ounces)

2 medium red **or** orange peppers, cut into 2-inch-long thin strips (about 3 cups)

2 medium zucchini, thinly sliced (about 3 cups)

1 medium onion, thinly sliced (about ½ cup)

12 **uncooked** no-boil lasagna noodles

2 cups shredded Monterey Jack cheese (8 ounces)

1. Stir the soup and milk in a small bowl and set aside. Spray a 13×9×2-inch shallow baking dish with cooking spray.

2. Heat the butter in a 12-inch skillet over medium heat. Add the mushrooms, peppers, zucchini and onion and cook until tender.

3. Spread **1 cup** soup mixture in the bottom of the prepared dish. Arrange **3** of the noodles and top with **one-third** of the vegetable mixture, **1 cup** of the soup mixture and ½ **cup** of the cheese. Repeat layers twice. Top with remaining 3 noodles. Pour remaining soup mixture over noodles. **Cover.**

4. Bake at 375°F. for 40 minutes. Uncover and sprinkle with remaining cheese. Bake for 10 minutes more or until hot. Let the lasagna stand for 10 minutes.

Turkey and Stuffing Casserole

MAKES 6 SERVINGS

PREP
5 minutes

BAKE
25 minutes

Vegetable cooking spray

1 can (10¾ ounces) Campbell's® Condensed Cream of Mushroom
   Soup (Regular, 98% Fat Free **or** 25% Less Sodium)

1 cup milk **or** water

1 bag (16 ounces) frozen vegetable combination (broccoli,
   cauliflower, carrots), thawed

2 cups cubed cooked turkey **or** chicken

4 cups Pepperidge Farm® Cubed Herb Seasoned Stuffing

1 cup shredded Swiss **or** Cheddar cheese (4 ounces)

EASY SUBSTITUTION TIP

*Substitute 1 can
(9.75 ounces)
Swanson® Premium
White Chunk Chicken
Breast, drained for
the cubed cooked
turkey.*

1. Spray a 12×8×2-inch shallow baking dish with cooking spray
and set aside.

2. Stir the soup and milk in a large bowl. Stir in the vegetables, turkey
and stuffing. Spoon the mixture into the prepared dish.

3. Bake at 400°F. for 20 minutes or until hot and bubbly. Stir.

4. Sprinkle the cheese over the turkey mixture. Bake for 5 minutes more
or until the cheese melts.

Ranchero Oven-Fried Chicken

PREP
10 minutes

BAKE
50 minutes

3 cups Pepperidge Farm® Herb Seasoned **or** Corn Bread Stuffing, crushed

½ cup all-purpose flour

1 can (10¾ ounces) Campbell's® Condensed Tomato Soup

½ cup mayonnaise

1 tablespoon water

1 teaspoon chili powder

½ teaspoon ground cumin

4 pounds chicken parts (breasts, thighs **and/or** drumsticks)*

COOKING FOR A CROWD

Recipe may be doubled. Double all ingredients.

1. Put the crushed stuffing and flour on 2 separate plates.

2. Stir the soup, mayonnaise, water, chili powder and cumin in a shallow dish. Lightly coat the chicken with the flour. Dip the chicken into the soup mixture, then coat with the stuffing. Put the chicken on a baking sheet.

3. Bake at 400°F. for 50 minutes or until the chicken is cooked through. Serve the chicken warm or at room temperature.

Make Ahead: Prepare the chicken as directed and cool for 30 minutes. Cover and refrigerate the chicken for up to 24 hours. When ready to serve, place the chicken on a baking sheet and bake at 350°F. for 30 minutes or until hot.

Remove skin if desired.

Braised Beef Short Ribs

PREP
20 minutes

COOK
1 hour 45 minutes

3 to 4 pounds beef short ribs, cut into serving-size pieces
Ground black pepper

1 tablespoon olive oil

2 stalks celery, coarsely chopped (about 1 cup)

1 large carrot, coarsely chopped (about 1 cup)

1 large onion, coarsely chopped (about 1 cup)

3 medium Italian plum tomatoes, chopped

3 cloves garlic, minced

1 cup Swanson® Beef Broth (Regular, Lower Sodium **or** Certified Organic)

½ cup dry red wine

2 tablespoons balsamic vinegar

1 tablespoon chopped fresh rosemary **or** 1 teaspoon dried rosemary leaves, crushed

1 bay leaf

2 tablespoons all-purpose flour

¼ cup water

TRANSPORTING TIP

After removing the cooked ribs from the skillet, cool slightly then cut the meat from the bones to make potluck dining easier.

1. Season the ribs with the black pepper. Heat the oil in a 12-inch skillet over medium-high heat. Add the ribs and cook until they're well browned on all sides. Remove the ribs.

2. Add the celery, carrot, onion, tomatoes and garlic and cook until tender. Add the broth, wine, vinegar, rosemary and bay leaf. Heat to a boil. Return the ribs to the skillet and reduce the heat to low. Cover and cook for 1 hour 15 minutes or until the ribs are cooked through.

3. Remove the ribs and keep warm. Stir the flour and water in a small cup and stir into the broth mixture. Cook and stir over medium-high heat until the mixture boils and thickens. Remove the bay leaf. Serve gravy with the ribs.

Cavatelli with Sausage & Broccoli

1   package (16 ounces) frozen cavatelli pasta

1   tablespoon olive oil

1   pound sweet Italian pork sausage, casing removed

1   tablespoon butter

2   cloves garlic, minced

1   bag (about 16 ounces) frozen broccoli flowerets

1¾ cups Swanson® Chicken Broth (Regular, Natural Goodness™ **or** Certified Organic)

Grated Romano cheese

Crushed red pepper

PREP
10 minutes

COOK
30 minutes

TRANSPORTING TIP

To keep moist, add some Swanson® Chicken Broth and stir in at step 5.

1. Cook the pasta according to the package directions. Drain well in a colander. Return the pasta to the saucepot.

2. Heat the oil in a 10-inch skillet over medium-high heat. Add the sausage and cook until it's well browned, stirring frequently to separate meat. Remove the sausage with a slotted spoon. Set aside.

3. Add the butter and garlic to the skillet. Cook over medium heat about 2 minutes or until golden.

4. Add the broccoli. Cook for 5 minutes until tender-crisp, stirring often. Stir the broth into the skillet. Heat to a boil. Remove from the heat.

5. Add the broccoli mixture, sausage and **2 tablespoons** cheese to the saucepot. Cook and stir over medium heat for 10 minutes or until the sauce thickens. Serve with the red pepper and additional cheese, if desired.

Sausage-Stuffed Green Peppers

MAKES 8 SERVINGS

PREP
20 minutes

BAKE
40 minutes

4   medium green peppers

1   tablespoon vegetable oil

1   pound sweet Italian pork sausage, casing removed

1   teaspoon dried oregano leaves, crushed

1   medium onion, chopped (about ½ cup)

1   cup shredded part-skim mozzarella cheese (4 ounces)

2   cups Prego® Traditional Italian Sauce

1. Cut a thin slice from the top of each pepper, cut in half lengthwise and discard the seeds and white membranes. Place the pepper shells in a 13×9×2-inch shallow baking dish or roasting pan and set them aside.

2. Heat the oil in a 10-inch skillet over medium-high heat. Add the sausage and cook until it's well browned, stirring to break up the meat. Add the oregano and onion and cook until the onion is tender. Pour off any fat. Stir in the cheese.

3. Spoon the sausage mixture into the pepper shells. Pour the Italian sauce over the peppers. **Cover**. Bake at 400°F. for 40 minutes or until sausage reaches an internal temperature of 160°F. and the peppers are tender.

Herbed Pork Roast & Creamy Mushroom Gravy

1 teaspoon **each** minced fresh rosemary, parsley **and** thyme **or**
   ¼ teaspoon **each** dried rosemary, parsley flakes **and** thyme
   leaves, crushed

1 clove garlic, minced

   2½- to 3-pound boneless pork loin roast

1 can (10¾ ounces) Campbell's® Condensed Cream of Mushroom
   Soup (Regular, 98% Fat Free **or** 25% Less Sodium)

½ cup water

PREP
10 minutes

BAKE
1 hour 30 minutes

STAND
10 minutes

1. Stir together the rosemary, parsley, thyme and garlic in a small bowl.
Cut small slits into the surface of the roast with a knife. Stuff the herb
mixture into the slits. Place the roast in a roasting pan.

2. Bake at 325°F. for 1 hour 30 minutes or until the pork is cooked
through. Remove the roast from the pan to a cutting board and let it
stand for 10 minutes.

3. Stir the soup into the pan drippings in the roasting pan. Gradually stir
in the water. Cook and stir over medium heat until the mixture is hot and
bubbling. Thinly slice the pork. Pour the gravy into a gravy boat and serve
it with the pork.

> **TRANSPORTING TIP**
>
> *Cut the thin slices of
> pork into bite-sized
> pieces to make
> potluck dining easier
> with just a fork.*

Savory Pot Roast

PREP
 10 minutes

COOK
 8 to 9 hours

TRANSPORTING TIP

Remove cooked roast and cut into bite-sized pieces to make potluck dining easier. Return cut pieces to soup mixture and take along in the slow cooker to keep warm at the potluck.

1 can (10¾ ounces) Campbell's® Condensed Cream of Mushroom Soup (Regular, 98% Fat Free **or** 25% Less Sodium)

1 pouch (1 ounce) Campbell's® Dry Onion Soup Mix

6 medium potatoes, cut into quarters

6 medium carrots, cut into 2-inch pieces

   3½- to 4-pound boneless beef bottom round **or** chuck pot roast

1. Stir the mushroom soup, onion soup mix, potatoes and carrots in a 3½-quart slow cooker. Top with the roast and turn to coat.

2. Cover and cook on LOW for 8 to 9 hours* or until the roast is fork-tender.

Or on HIGH for 4 to 5 hours

Quick Skillet Chicken & Macaroni Parmesan

MAKES 6 SERVINGS

Ingredients	Timing

1   jar (1 pound 10 ounces) Prego® Traditional Italian Sauce
    or Prego® Organic Tomato & Basil Italian Sauce

3   cups shredded cooked chicken

1   cup elbow macaroni, cooked and drained

¼   cup grated Parmesan cheese

1½ cups shredded part-skim mozzarella cheese (6 ounces)

PREP
10 minutes

COOK
15 minutes

STAND
5 minutes

1. Heat the sauce in a 12-inch skillet over medium-high heat. Heat to a boil. Add the chicken, macaroni and **3 tablespoons** of the Parmesan cheese. Reduce the heat to low and cook for 5 minutes or until heated through.

2. Sprinkle the mozzarella cheese and remaining Parmesan cheese over the chicken and macaroni. Let stand for 5 minutes or until the cheese melts.

Soups, Chilis & More

The always-perfect food for a crowd

Bacon Potato Chowder

PREP
15 minutes

COOK
30 minutes

4   slices bacon

1   large onion, chopped (about 1 cup)

4   cans (10¾ ounces **each**) Campbell's® Condensed Cream
    of Potato Soup

4   soup cans milk

¼   teaspoon ground black pepper

2   large russet potatoes, cut into ½-inch pieces (about 3 cups)

2   cups shredded Cheddar cheese (8 ounces)

½   cup chopped fresh chives

*Transfer the chowder
to a slow cooker.
Chowder tends to
thicken upon standing,
so bring along some
Swanson® Vegetable
or Chicken Broth to
stir in before serving.*

1. Cook bacon in 6-quart saucepot over medium-high heat until it's crisp.
Remove bacon with a fork and drain on paper towels. Crumble the
bacon.

2. Add the onion and cook in the hot drippings until tender.

3. Stir the soup, milk, black pepper and potatoes into the saucepot.
Heat to a boil. Reduce the heat to low. Cover and cook for 15 minutes
or until the potatoes are tender. Remove from the heat.

4. Add the cheese and stir until the cheese melts. Serve with the chives.

Beef 'n' Brew Stew

PREP
25 minutes

BAKE
2 hours

3 tablespoons vegetable oil

3 pounds boneless beef chuck cut into 1-inch pieces

2 large onions, sliced (about 2 cups)

2 cloves garlic, minced

2 cans (10¾ ounces **each**) Campbell's® Condensed Golden Mushroom Soup

2 cans (10½ ounces **each**) Campbell's® Condensed French Onion Soup

1 bottle (12 fluid ounces) dark beer **or** stout

1 tablespoon packed brown sugar

1 tablespoon cider vinegar

½ teaspoon dried thyme leaves, crushed

1 bay leaf

2 cups fresh **or** frozen baby carrots

Egg noodles, cooked, drained and buttered

1. Heat **1 tablespoon** of the oil in an oven-safe 6-quart saucepot over medium-high heat. Add the beef in 3 batches and cook until it's well browned, stirring often. (Add **1 tablespoon** of oil as needed.) Remove the beef with a slotted spoon and set aside.

2. Reduce the heat to medium. Add remaining oil and heat. Add the onions and garlic and cook until tender.

3. Stir the soups, beer, brown sugar, vinegar, thyme, bay leaf and carrots into the saucepot. Heat to a boil.

4. Cover the saucepot and bake at 300°F. for 2 hours or until the meat is fork-tender. Remove the bay leaf. Serve stew over the noodles.

Sausage and Bean Ragoût

PREP
10 minutes

COOK
20 minutes

2   tablespoons olive oil

1   pound ground beef

1   pound hot Italian pork sausage, casing removed

1   large onion, chopped (1 cup)

4   cloves garlic, minced

3½ cups Swanson® Chicken Broth (Regular, Natural Goodness™ **or** Certified Organic)

¼   cup chopped fresh basil

2   cans (14½ ounces **each**) diced tomatoes seasoned with garlic, oregano and basil

1   can (about 16 ounces) white kidney (cannellini) beans, rinsed and drained

½   cup **uncooked** elbow pasta

1   bag (6 ounces) baby spinach leaves, washed

⅓   cup grated Romano cheese

1. Heat the oil in a 6-quart saucepot over medium-high heat. Add the beef, sausage and onion and cook until the meats are well browned, stirring frequently to break up meat. Add the garlic and cook for 30 seconds.

2. Stir the broth, basil, tomatoes and beans into the saucepot. Heat to a boil. Reduce the heat to low. Cover and cook for 10 minutes, stirring occasionally. Add the pasta and cook until pasta is done.

3. Add the spinach and cook just until spinach wilts, stirring occasionally. Remove from the heat and stir in the cheese. Serve with additional cheese.

Creamy Chicken Tortilla Soup

PREP
15 minutes

COOK
5 hours
15 minutes

1 cup Pace® Chunky Salsa

1 pound skinless, boneless chicken breasts, cut into ½-inch pieces

2 cups frozen whole kernel corn

1 can (about 15 ounces) black beans, rinsed and drained

2 cans (10¾ ounces **each**) Campbell's® Condensed Cream of Chicken Soup

1 soup can water

1 teaspoon ground cumin

4 corn tortillas (6-inch), cut into strips

1 cup shredded Cheddar cheese

⅓ cup chopped fresh cilantro leaves

1. Stir the salsa, chicken, corn and beans in a 4-quart slow cooker.

2. Stir the soup, water and cumin in a small bowl. Pour over the chicken mixture.

3. Cover and cook on LOW for 5 hours*.

4. Stir the tortillas, **1 cup** of the cheese and cilantro into the cooker. Cover and cook for 15 minutes more. Serve with additional cheese, if desired.

*Or on HIGH for 2 to 2½ hours

Chicken & Tortellini Stew

PREP
10 minutes

COOK
35 minutes

1   tablespoon cornstarch

1   tablespoon water

2   tablespoons vegetable oil

¾   pound skinless, boneless chicken breasts, cut into cubes

¾   cup chopped onions

1   cup frozen sliced carrots

1   cup frozen cut green beans

6   cups Swanson® Chicken Broth (Regular, Natural Goodness™ **or** Certified Organic)

1   cup dried cheese-filled tortellini

2   tablespoons chopped fresh parsley

1. Stir the cornstarch and water in a small cup until smooth. Set aside.

2. Heat **1 tablespoon** of the oil in a 6-quart saucepot over medium-high heat. Add the chicken and cook until it's well browned, stirring often. Remove the chicken.

3. Add the remaining oil. Add onions, carrots and beans. Cook over medium heat until tender-crisp.

4. Stir the broth into the saucepot. Heat to a boil. Add the tortellini and parsley. Cook for 10 minutes or until the tortellini is tender. Return the chicken to the saucepot and heat through.

5. Stir the cornstarch mixture and add. Cook until mixture boils and thickens slightly.

Spicy Verde Chicken & Bean Chili

PREP
10 minutes

COOK
40 minutes

2 tablespoons butter

1 large onion, chopped (about 1 cup)

¼ teaspoon garlic powder **or** 2 cloves garlic, minced

1 tablespoon all-purpose flour

2 cups Swanson® Chicken Broth (Regular, Natural Goodness™ **or** Certified Organic)

2 cups shredded cooked chicken

1 can (about 16 ounces) small white beans, undrained

1 can (4 ounces) chopped green chilies, drained

1 teaspoon ground cumin

1 teaspoon jalapeño hot pepper sauce

6 flour tortillas (8-inch), warmed

Shredded Monterey Jack cheese (optional)

Chopped fresh cilantro (optional)

1. Heat the butter in a 12-inch skillet over medium heat. Add the onion and garlic powder. Cook and stir until the onion is tender.

2. Stir in the flour. Cook and stir for 2 minutes. Slowly stir in the broth. Cook and stir until the mixture boils and thickens.

3. Stir in the chicken, beans, chilies, cumin and hot sauce. Heat to a boil. Reduce the heat to low. Cook for 20 minutes, stirring occasionally.

4. Line 6 serving bowls with the tortillas. Divide the chili among the bowls. Serve topped with cheese and cilantro, if desired.

West African Vegetable Stew

PREP
15 minutes

COOK
30 minutes

1 tablespoon vegetable oil

2 cups sliced onions

2 cloves garlic, minced

2 sweet potatoes (about 1½ pounds), peeled and cut in half lengthwise and sliced

1 large tomato, coarsely chopped (1½ cups)

1 can (10½ ounces) Campbell's® Condensed Chicken Broth

½ cup water

½ teaspoon **each** ground cinnamon **and** crushed red pepper

½ cup raisins

4 cups coarsely chopped fresh spinach leaves

1 can (about 15 ounces) chickpeas (garbanzo beans), rinsed and drained

Cooked rice **or** couscous, optional

1. Heat the oil in a 6-quart saucepot over medium heat. Add the onion and garlic and cook until tender.

2. Add the potatoes and tomatoes. Cook for 5 minutes.

3. Stir the broth, water, cinnamon, red pepper and raisins into the saucepot. Heat to a boil. Reduce the heat to low. Cover and cook for 15 minutes.

4. Add the spinach and chickpeas. Heat through. Serve over rice or couscous, if desired.

Herb-Simmered Beef Stew

PREP
15 minutes

COOK
1 hour 30 minutes

2 pounds beef for stew, cut into 1-inch pieces

Ground black pepper

2 tablespoons all-purpose flour

2 tablespoons olive oil

3 cups thickly sliced mushrooms (about 8 ounces)

3 cloves garlic, minced

½ teaspoon **each** dried marjoram, thyme **and** rosemary leaves, crushed **or** 1½ teaspoons **each** chopped fresh marjoram, thyme **and** rosemary

1 bay leaf

1¾ cups Swanson® Beef Broth (Regular, Lower Sodium **or** Certified Organic)

3 cups fresh **or** frozen baby carrots

12 whole baby red-skinned potatoes, with a strip of peel removed in center

1. Sprinkle the beef with the black pepper and coat with the flour.

2. Heat the oil in a 6-quart saucepot over medium-high heat. Add the beef and cook until it's well browned, stirring often.

3. Add the mushrooms, garlic, herbs and bay leaf and cook until the mushrooms are tender and liquid evaporates.

4. Stir the broth into the saucepot. Heat to a boil. Reduce the heat to low. Cover and cook for 45 minutes.

5. Add the carrots and potatoes. Heat to a boil. Cover and cook for 30 minutes more or until the beef is fork-tender. Remove the bay leaf.

Hearty Bean & Barley Soup

MAKES 6 SERVINGS

1	tablespoon olive oil
2	large carrots, coarsely chopped (about 1 cup)
2	stalks celery, sliced (about 1 cup)
1	large onion, chopped (about 1 cup)
3	cloves garlic, minced
3½	cups Swanson® Vegetable Broth (Regular **or** Certified Organic)
1	can (about 15 ounces) red kidney beans, drained and rinsed
1	can (14½ ounces) diced tomatoes
¼	cup **uncooked** pearl barley
2	cups firmly packed chopped fresh spinach leaves
	Ground black pepper

PREP
15 minutes

COOK
40 minutes

1. Heat the oil in a 4-quart saucepan over medium-high heat. Add the carrots, celery, onion and garlic. Cook and stir until the vegetables are tender.

2. Stir the broth, beans, tomatoes and barley into the saucepan. Heat to a boil. Reduce the heat to low. Cover and cook for 30 minutes or until the barley is done.

3. Stir in the spinach and season to taste with black pepper. Heat through.

Picante Pork Stew

PREP
20 minutes

COOK
25 minutes

2 pounds boneless pork loin

6 tablespoons cornstarch

3½ cups Swanson® Vegetable Broth (Regular **or** Certified Organic)

¼ cup vegetable oil

8 cups cut-up fresh vegetables (asparagus, cut into 2-inch pieces, red pepper cut into 2-inch-long strips and sliced onions)

1 cup Pace® Picante Sauce

1. Slice the pork into very thin strips. Stir the cornstarch and broth in a medium bowl until smooth. Set aside.

2. Heat **1 tablespoon** of the oil in a 6-quart saucepot over medium-high heat. Add the pork and cook in 2 batches until it's well browned, stirring often. Set the pork aside.

3. Add the remaining oil and heat over medium heat. Add the vegetables and cook until tender-crisp. Pour off fat.

4. Stir the picante sauce into the saucepot. Stir cornstarch mixture and add. Cook until the mixture boils and thickens, stirring constantly. Return the pork to the saucepot and heat through.

Roasted Tomato & Barley Soup

MAKES 8 SERVINGS

1   can (28 ounces) diced tomatoes, undrained

2   large onions, diced (about 2 cups)

2   cloves garlic, minced

2   tablespoons olive oil

4   cups Swanson® Chicken Broth (Regular, Natural Goodness™ **or** Certified Organic)

2   stalks celery, diced (about 1 cup)

½   cup **uncooked** barley

2   tablespoons chopped fresh parsley

PREP
10 minutes

BAKE
25 minutes

COOK
40 minutes

1. Heat the oven to 425°F. Drain the tomatoes, reserving the juice. Put the tomatoes, onions and garlic in a 17×11-inch roasting pan. Pour the oil over the vegetables and toss to coat. Bake for 25 minutes.

2. Put the roasted vegetables in a 3-quart saucepan. Add the reserved tomato juice, broth, celery and barley and heat to a boil. Cover and reduce the heat to low.

3. Cook for 35 minutes or until the barley is tender. Stir in the parsley.

Make-Ahead Sides & Salads

Just heat or toss together right

before serving

Squash Casserole

PREP
15 minutes

BAKE
40 minutes

3 cups Pepperidge Farm® Corn Bread Stuffing

¼ cup butter, melted

1 can (10¾ ounces) Campbell's® Cream of Chicken Soup
  (Regular **or** 98% Fat Free)

½ cup sour cream

2 small yellow squash, shredded (about 2 cups)

2 small zucchini, shredded (about 2 cups)

¼ cup shredded carrot

½ cup shredded Cheddar cheese

1. Mix stuffing and butter in bowl. Reserve ½ **cup** of stuffing mixture for topping. Spoon remaining stuffing mixture into 12×8×2-inch shallow baking dish.

2. Stir soup, sour cream, yellow squash, zucchini, carrot and cheese in bowl. Spread vegetable mixture over stuffing mixture. Sprinkle with reserved stuffing mixture.

3. Bake at 350°F. for 40 minutes or until hot and topping is golden.

Broccoli 'n' Cheese Casserole

MAKES 6 SERVINGS

PREP
5 minutes

BAKE
30 minutes

Vegetable cooking spray

1 can (10¾ ounces) Campbell's® Condensed Cream of Mushroom Soup (Regular, 98% Fat Free **or** 25% Less Sodium)

½ cup milk

1 tablespoon Dijon-style mustard

1 bag (16 ounces) frozen broccoli flowerets, thawed (about 4 cups) **or** your favorite vegetable

1 cup shredded Cheddar cheese (4 ounces)

1 cup Italian-seasoned dry bread crumbs

2 tablespoons butter, melted

1. Spray a 2-quart casserole with cooking spray. Stir the soup, milk, mustard, broccoli and cheese in the prepared dish.

2. Mix the bread crumbs and the butter in a small bowl and sprinkle over the broccoli mixture.

3. Bake at 350°F. for 30 minutes or until hot and bubbly.

Loaded Baked Potato Casserole

PREP
15 minutes

BAKE
35 minutes

1 bag (32 ounces) frozen Southern-style hash brown potatoes, thawed (about 7½ cups)

1 can (6 ounces) French fried onions (2⅔ cups)

1 cup frozen peas, thawed

1 cup shredded Cheddar cheese (4 ounces)

4 slices bacon, cooked and crumbled

2 cans (10¾ ounces **each**) Campbell's® Condensed Cream of Celery Soup (Regular **or** 98% Fat Free)

1 cup milk

TIME-SAVING TIP

To thaw the hash browns, cut off 1 corner on bag, microwave on HIGH for 5 minutes.

1. Stir the potatoes, **1⅓ cups** of the onions, peas, cheese and bacon in a 13×9×2-inch shallow baking dish. Stir the soup and milk in a medium bowl and pour over the potato mixture. **Cover**.

2. Bake at 350°F. for 30 minutes or until hot. Stir the potato mixture.

3. Sprinkle the remaining onions over the potato mixture. Bake for 5 minutes more or until the onions are golden brown.

Golden Onions & Spinach Bake

MAKES 8 SERVINGS

1   can (10¾ ounces) Campbell's® Condensed Cream
    of Celery Soup (Regular **or** 98% Fat Free)

¼   cup sour cream

2   tablespoons grated Parmesan cheese

¼   teaspoon ground nutmeg

2   packages (about 10 ounces **each**) frozen chopped spinach,
    thawed and drained

1   can (2.8 ounces) French fried onions (1⅓ cups)

PREP
5 minutes

BAKE
25 minutes

1. Stir the soup, sour cream, cheese, nutmeg, spinach and ⅔ **cup** onions
in a 1½-quart casserole. **Cover.**

2. Bake at 350°F. for 20 minutes. Stir the spinach mixture.

3. Sprinkle the remaining onions over the spinach mixture. Bake for
5 minutes more or until the onions are golden brown.

TIME-SAVING TIP

*To thaw the spinach,
microwave on
HIGH for 3 minutes,
breaking apart with a
fork halfway through
heating.*

Ultimate Mashed Potatoes

PREP
5 minutes

COOK
20 minutes

3½ cups Swanson® Chicken Broth (Regular, Natural Goodness™
     or Certified Organic)

5 large potatoes, cut into 1-inch pieces

½ cup light cream

2 tablespoons butter

   Generous dash ground black pepper

3 slices bacon, cooked and crumbled

½ cup sour cream

¼ cup chopped fresh chives

1. Heat the broth and potatoes in a 3-quart saucepan over medium-high heat to a boil.

2. Reduce the heat to medium. Cover and cook for 10 minutes or until the potatoes are tender. Drain, reserving the broth.

3. Mash potatoes with ¼ **cup** of the reserved broth, cream, butter and black pepper.

4. Reserve **1 tablespoon** of the crumbled bacon. Stir the remaining bacon, sour cream and chives into the potatoes. Add additional broth, if needed, until desired consistency. Sprinkle with the reserved bacon.

Swiss Vegetable Casserole

1   can (10¾ ounces) Campbell's® Cream of Mushroom Soup
    (Regular, 98% Fat Free **or** 25% Less Sodium)

⅓   cup sour cream

¼   teaspoon ground black pepper

1   bag (16 ounces) frozen vegetable combination (broccoli,
    cauliflower, carrots), thawed

1   can (2.8 ounces) French fried onions (1⅓ cups)

½   cup shredded Swiss cheese

PREP
5 minutes

BAKE
45 minutes

1. Stir the soup, sour cream, black pepper, vegetables, ⅔ **cup** of the onions and ¼ **cup** of the cheese in a 2-quart casserole. **Cover.**

2. Bake at 350°F. for 40 minutes or until the vegetables are tender. Stir the vegetable mixture.

3. Sprinkle the remaining onions and cheese over the vegetable mixture. Bake for 5 minutes more or until the onions are golden brown.

> **COOKING FOR A CROWD**
>
> *Recipe may be doubled. Double all ingredients.*

Green Bean Casserole

PREP
10 minutes

BAKE
30 minutes

2 cans (10¾ ounces **each**) Campbell's® Condensed Cream of Mushroom Soup (Regular, 98% Fat Free **or** 25% Less Sodium)

1 cup milk

2 teaspoons soy sauce

¼ teaspoon ground black pepper

8 cups cooked cut green beans

1 can (6 ounces) French fried onions (2⅔ cups)

EASY SUBSTITUTION TIP

*You can make this classic side dish with fresh, frozen **or** canned green beans. You will need either 1½ pounds fresh green beans, cut into 1-inch pieces, cooked and drained, **or** 2 cans (about 16 ounces **each**) cut green beans, drained, **or** 8 cups frozen green beans.*

1. Stir the soup, milk, soy sauce, black pepper, green beans and **1⅓ cups** onions in a 3-quart casserole.

2. Bake at 350°F. for 25 minutes or until hot. Stir the green bean mixture.

3. Sprinkle the remaining onions over the green bean mixture. Bake for 5 minutes more or until onions are golden brown.

Layered Cranberry Walnut Stuffing

2   boxes (6 ounces **each**) Pepperidge Farm® Stuffing Mix

1½ cups Swanson® Chicken Broth (Regular, Natural Goodness™
      or Certified Organic)

2   tablespoons butter

1   can (16 ounces) whole cranberry sauce

½   cup walnuts, toasted and chopped

PREP
10 minutes

BAKE
25 minutes

1. Prepare the stuffing using the broth and butter according to the package directions.

2. Spoon **half** of the stuffing into a 2-quart casserole. Spoon **half** of the cranberry sauce over the stuffing. Sprinkle with ¼ **cup** walnuts. Repeat the layers.

3. Bake at 350°F. for 25 minutes or until hot.

Onion Gratin

PREP
20 minutes

BAKE
45 minutes

TIME-SAVING TIP

Cut off the ends of the onions and place them in a bowl. Pour boiling water over the onions and let stand for 5 minutes. Pour off the water and then slip the skin off the onions.

2   pounds small whole white onions (about 30 to 32), peeled

1   can (10¾ ounces) Campbell's® Condensed Cream of Mushroom Soup (Regular, 98% Fat Free **or** 25% Less Sodium)

¾   cup milk

1¼   cups shredded Cheddar cheese (about 5 ounces)

½   cup crushed corn flakes

1. Arrange the onions in a 12×8×2-inch shallow baking dish.

2. Stir the soup, milk and ¼ **cup** of the cheese in a small bowl and pour over the onions.

3. Mix the corn flake crumbs with the remaining cheese in a small bowl and sprinkle over the onions.

4. Bake at 350°F. for 45 minutes or until hot and bubbly and the onions are tender.

Lemon Herb Broccoli Casserole

MAKES 6 SERVINGS

1   can (10¾ ounces) Campbell's® Condensed Cream
    of Chicken with Herbs Soup

½   cup milk

1   tablespoon lemon juice

1   bag (16 ounces) frozen broccoli cuts, thawed (about 4 cups)

1   can (2.8 ounces) French fried onions (1⅓ cups)

PREP
10 minutes

BAKE
30 minutes

1. Stir the soup, milk, lemon juice, broccoli and ⅔ **cup** of the onions
in a 1½-quart casserole.

2. Bake at 350°F. for 25 minutes or until the broccoli is tender. Stir the
broccoli mixture.

3. Sprinkle the remaining onions over the broccoli mixture. Bake for
5 minutes more or until the onions are golden brown.

Toasted Corn & Sage Harvest Risotto

PREP
15 minutes

COOK
35 minutes

EASY SUBSTITUTION TIP

*If you want a meatless side dish, substitute Swanson® Vegetable Broth (Regular, Natural Goodness™ **or** Certified Organic) for the chicken broth.*

1 tablespoon olive oil

1 cup fresh **or** drained, canned whole kernel corn

1 large orange **or** red pepper, chopped (about 1 cup)

1 medium onion, chopped (about ½ cup)

1¾ cups **uncooked** regular long-grain white rice

4 cups Swanson® Chicken Broth (Regular, Natural Goodness™ **or** Certified Organic)

1 teaspoon ground sage

1 can (10¾ ounces) Campbell's® Condensed Cream of Celery Soup (Regular **or** 98% Fat Free)

¼ cup grated Parmesan cheese

1. Heat the oil in a 4-quart saucepan over medium heat. Add the corn, pepper and onion and cook for 6 minutes or until the vegetables start to brown.

2. Add the rice and cook for 30 seconds, stirring constantly. Stir in the broth and sage and heat to a boil. Reduce the heat to low. Cover the saucepan and cook for 20 minutes or until the rice is done and most of the liquid is absorbed.

3. Stir in the soup. Cook for 2 minutes more, stirring occasionally until heated through. Sprinkle with cheese.

Creamy Corn Pudding

MAKES 6 SERVINGS

Butter

1   can (10¾ ounces) Campbell's® Condensed Cream of Chicken
      Soup (Regular **or** 98% Fat Free)

½   cup milk

2   eggs

1   can (16 ounces) whole kernel corn, drained

½   cup cornmeal

¼   cup grated Parmesan cheese

1   tablespoon chopped fresh chives

PREP
10 minutes

BAKE
35 minutes

1. Heat the oven to 350°F. Grease a 1½-quart casserole with butter.

2. Stir the soup, milk and eggs in a medium bowl. Stir in the corn, cornmeal, cheese and chives. Pour the soup mixture into the prepared casserole.

3. Bake for 35 minutes or until puffed and golden brown.

Cheesy Garlic Mashed Potatoes

PREP
50 minutes

BAKE
35 minutes

2 whole garlic bulbs

4 teaspoons vegetable oil

5⅓ cups instant mashed potatoes (buds **or** flakes)

5⅓ cups water

4 cups milk

1 stick (½ cup) butter

1 container (16 ounces) sour cream

3 cups shredded white Cheddar cheese (12 ounces)

2 cans (10½ ounces **each**) Campbell's® Brown Gravy with Onions

TRANSPORTING TIP

Heat the gravy and pour into a thermos to keep it hot.

1. Place the garlic bulbs on a piece of foil. Drizzle with the vegetable oil and wrap in the foil. Bake at 350°F. for 45 minutes or until the garlic is soft. Squeeze the soft garlic from the garlic skin into a bowl. Set aside.

2. Prepare the potatoes using the water, milk and butter according to the package directions, omitting the salt. Stir in the roasted garlic and sour cream.

3. Spoon **half** of the potato mixture into each of **2** (2-quart) casseroles. Sprinkle each with **1 cup** of the cheese. Top with the remaining potato mixture.

4. Bake at 350°F. for 30 minutes or until hot. Sprinkle with the remaining cheese. Bake for 5 minutes more or until cheese melts.

5. Heat the gravy according to the package directions. Serve with the potatoes.

Broth Simmered Rice

MAKES 4 SERVINGS

1¾　cups Swanson® Chicken Broth (Regular, Natural Goodness™ **or** Certified Organic)

¾　cup **uncooked** regular long-grain white rice

1. Heat the broth in a 2-quart saucepan over medium-high heat to a boil.

2. Stir in the rice. Reduce the heat to low. Cover the saucepan and cook for 20 minutes or until the rice is tender and most of the liquid is absorbed.

Cooking for a Crowd: Recipe may be doubled. Double all ingredients.

PREP
5 minutes

COOK
25 minutes

EASY SUBSTITUTION TIP

*Substitute Swanson® Beef **or** Vegetable **or** Seasoned Broths for the Chicken Broth.*

Have Dessert, Will Travel

Party-pleasing sweets that will win over

any crowd

Raspberry Tiramisu Trifle

MAKES 18 SERVINGS

PREP
20 minutes

REFRIGERATE
1 hour

3   packages (8 ounces **each**) cream cheese, softened

3   cups confectioners' sugar

¾   teaspoon ground cinnamon

3   cups heavy cream, whipped

2   packages (6 ounces **each**) Pepperidge Farm® Milano®
    Distinctive Cookies

1   cup brewed black coffee

1⅓   cups fresh **or** frozen sweetened raspberries, thawed and drained

¼   cup grated semi-sweet chocolate for garnish

TIME-SAVING TIP

Heavy cream will whip faster when the bowl and beaters are cold. Place the bowl and beaters in the freezer for about 15 minutes before using, then use the cream right from the refrigerator when you're ready to beat.

1. Beat the cream cheese in a large bowl with an electric mixer on medium speed until smooth. Beat in the sugar and cinnamon. Stir in the whipped cream.

2. Spoon about **2 cups** of the cheese mixture into an 8-cup trifle bowl. Dip **9** of the cookies, one at a time, into the coffee and place over the cheese layer, overlapping slightly. Spoon ⅓ **cup** of the raspberries over the cookies. Repeat the layers twice. Spread the remaining cheese mixture over the top. Garnish with the remaining cookies and raspberries. Refrigerate for at least 1 hour.

3. Garnish with the chocolate before serving.

Baked Pumpkin Custard Tarts

PREP
15 minutes

BAKE
50 minutes

COOL
50 minutes

Vegetable cooking spray

½ cup sugar

1 teaspoon cornstarch

1 teaspoon ground cinnamon

¼ teaspoon ground cloves

1 can (15 ounces) pumpkin pie mix (1½ cups)

1 can (12 ounces) evaporated milk

4 eggs

2 tablespoons milk

2 packages (10 ounces **each**) Pepperidge Farm® Frozen Puff Pastry Shells

Sweetened whipped cream

Pumpkin pie spice for garnish

TRANSPORTING TIP

Transport the baked shells, pumpkin custard and whipped cream separately and fill tarts at the potluck.

1. Heat the oven to 325°F. Spray a 9-inch pie plate with cooking spray and set aside.

2. Mix the sugar, cornstarch, cinnamon and cloves in a large bowl. Stir in the pumpkin pie mix, evaporated milk, eggs and milk into the sugar mixture. Pour the pumpkin mixture into the prepared dish.

3. Bake for 50 minutes or until a knife inserted in the center comes out clean. Cool on a wire rack.

4. Bake and cool the pastry shells according to the package directions. Spoon ⅓ **cup** of the pumpkin custard into each shell. Top with whipped cream and sprinkle with pumpkin pie spice.

Bread Pudding with Pecan Caramel Sauce

MAKES 6 SERVINGS

PREP
30 minutes

BAKE
50 minutes

STAND
15 minutes

Butter

4 eggs

2 cups sugar

1 cup milk

1 teaspoon vanilla extract

1 loaf (16 ounces) Pepperidge Farm® White Bread, cut into cubes (about 8 cups)

½ cup water

¾ cup heavy cream

1 cup pecans, toasted and chopped

1. Heat the oven to 325°F. Grease a 2-quart casserole with butter.

2. Beat the eggs and ½ **cup** of the sugar. Beat in the milk and vanilla. Add the bread and stir to coat. Let the mixture stand for 20 minutes, stirring occasionally or until the milk is absorbed. Pour the bread mixture into the prepared casserole.

3. Bake for 50 minutes or until the center is set. Let cool on a wire rack.

4. Place the remaining sugar and water in a heavy 2-quart saucepan. Stir gently to mix. Heat to a boil. Reduce the heat to low. *Do not stir.* Continue cooking until the sugar is golden brown.

5. Stir in cream gradually until blended (mixture can appear to form a thick mass or "seize", but it will blend). Stir in the pecans. Let stand for at least 15 minutes. Serve pudding with pecan sauce.

Mini Chocolate Cookie Cheesecakes

MAKES 16 SERVINGS

PREP
20 minutes

BAKE
20 minutes

COOL
1 hour

REFRIGERATE
2 hours

16 foil baking cups (2½-inch)

2 packages (4.9 ounces **each**) Pepperidge Farm® Mini Milano® Distinctive Cookies

2 packages (8 ounces **each**) cream cheese, softened

½ cup sugar

2 eggs

½ teaspoon vanilla extract

1. Heat the oven to 350°F. Put the foil baking cups into 16 (2½-inch) muffin-pan cups or on a baking sheet. Place **2** cookies in the bottom of each cup and set aside. Cut the remaining cookies in half.

2. Beat the cream cheese, sugar, eggs and vanilla in a medium bowl with an electric mixer on medium speed until smooth. Spoon the cheese mixture into the baking cups filling each cup ¾ full. Insert **2** cookie halves, with the cut ends down, into the cheese mixture of each cup.

3. Bake for 20 minutes or until the centers are set. Cool the cheesecakes on a wire rack for 1 hour. Refrigerate the cheesecakes for at least 2 hours before serving.

EASY SUBSTITUTION TIP

For a refreshing flavor, use the Pepperidge Farm® Mini Mint Milano® Cookies instead of the regular ones.

Lemon Cheesecake Tartlets

THAW
40 minutes

PREP
10 minutes

BAKE
10 minutes

COOL
30 minutes

REFRIGERATE
10 minutes

½ of a 17.3-ounce package Pepperidge Farm® Frozen Puff Pastry
   Sheets (1 sheet)

1 egg, beaten

½ of an 8-ounce package cream cheese, softened

½ cup lemon curd

½ cup thawed frozen whipped topping

   Fresh raspberries **or** blueberries

1. Thaw the pastry sheet at room temperature for 40 minutes or until it's easy to handle. Heat the oven to 375°F. Lightly grease 36 (1½-inch) mini-muffin pan cups.

2. Unfold the pastry sheet on a lightly floured surface. Roll into a 12×12-inch square. Cut pastry into 36 (2-inch) squares. Press the squares into the prepared muffin pan cups. Brush the top edges of pastry with the egg and prick center with a fork.

3. Bake for 10 minutes or until golden. Immediately press handle end of wooden spoon into center of each shell to make an indentation. Cool in pans on wire racks for 5 minutes. Remove pastry cups from pans and cool completely on wire racks.

4. Beat the cream cheese in medium bowl with an electric mixer on medium speed until it's smooth. Beat in the lemon curd. Stir in the whipped topping.

5. Pipe or spoon about **1 to 1½ teaspoons** cheese mixture into each pastry cup. Refrigerate for at least 10 minutes before serving or up to 1 day ahead. Top each with a raspberry or blueberry.

Red Devil's Chocolate Cake

PREP
15 minutes

BAKE
35 minutes

COOL
40 minutes

Vegetable cooking spray

2½ cups all-purpose flour

½ cup unsweetened cocoa

1½ teaspoons baking soda

¼ teaspoon salt

1 stick (½ cup) butter, softened

1¾ cups sugar

2 eggs

1 teaspoon vanilla extract

3 teaspoons grated orange peel

1½ cups Campbell's® Tomato Juice

Creamy Orange Butter Frosting

1 cup sweetened coconut, toasted

TRANSPORTING TIP

Put the cooled toasted coconut in a sealable plastic bag and sprinkle on the cake just before serving at the potluck.

---

1. Heat the oven to 350°F. Spray an 11¾×9⅜×½-inch disposable aluminum pan or a 13×9×2-inch baking pan with cooking spray. Set aside.

2. Mix the flour, cocoa, baking soda and salt in a medium bowl.

3. Beat the butter and sugar in a medium bowl with an electric mixer at medium speed until they're light and fluffy, occasionally scraping side of bowl. Beat in the eggs, one at a time, beating well after each addition. Beat in the vanilla and **1 teaspoon** of the orange peel. Reserve the remaining peel for the frosting.

4. Reduce the speed to low. Add the flour mixture alternately with the tomato juice, beginning and ending with the flour mixture. Beat well after each addition, occasionally scraping bowl. Pour the batter into the prepared pan.

5. Bake for 30 to 35 minutes or until a toothpick inserted in center comes out clean. Cool the cake in the pan on a wire rack. Frost with *Creamy Orange Butter Frosting* and sprinkle with the coconut. Store the cake in the refrigerator.

Creamy Orange Butter Frosting

6 tablespoons butter, softened

2 cups confectioners' sugar

2 tablespoons milk

¼ teaspoon vanilla extract

⅛ teaspoon salt

Put the butter, sugar, milk, vanilla, salt and reserved orange peel in a medium bowl. Beat with an electric mixer at low speed until smooth. Increase the speed to medium, adding a little more milk if necessary, to make the frosting more spreadable. **Makes 1½ cups**.

Tomato Soup Spice Cupcakes

PREP
10 minutes

BAKE
20 minutes

1 box (about 18 ounces) spice cake mix

1 can (10¾ ounces) Campbell's® Condensed Tomato Soup

½ cup water

2 eggs

Cream cheese frosting

1. Heat the oven to 350°F. Put baking cup liners into 24 (3-inch) muffin-pan cups or grease and flour cups.

2. Stir the cake mix, soup, water and eggs according to the package directions. Spoon the batter evenly into the prepared muffin-pan cups.

3. Bake for 20 minutes or until a toothpick inserted in the center of a cupcake comes out clean. Cool in the pans for 10 minutes on a wire rack.

4. Remove from the pans and cool completely. Frost with your favorite cream cheese frosting.

Cappuccino Praline Puffs

PREP
15 minutes

BAKE
30 minutes

COOL
30 minutes

REFRIGERATE
1 hour

1   package (10 ounces) Pepperidge Farm® Frozen Puff Pastry Shells

2   bars (1 ounce **each**) dark chocolate

2   teaspoons instant espresso powder **or** granules

1   teaspoon water

1   cup heavy cream

1   tablespoon sugar

½   cup candy toffee bits

    Ground cinnamon

EASY SUBSTITUTION TIP

Omit the heavy cream and sugar. Use 2 cups thawed frozen whipped topping.

1. Heat the oven to 400°F. Bake and cool the pastry shells according to the package directions.

2. Finely chop **1** chocolate bar. Shave the remaining chocolate bar with a vegetable peeler to make chocolate curls. Set aside.

3. Stir the espresso powder and water in a medium bowl until dissolved. Add the cream and sugar. Beat with an electric mixer at high speed until stiff peaks form. Fold the toffee bits and the chopped chocolate into the cream.

4. Divide the mixture among the pastry shells. Sift the cinnamon over the filling and top with the chocolate curls. Cover and refrigerate the shells for at least 1 hour before serving.

index

93